NEPAL 2016 HUMAN RIGHTS REPORT

EXECUTIVE SUMMARY

Nepal is a federal democratic republic. The political system is based on the constitution, which was promulgated in September 2015, replacing the Interim Constitution of Nepal 2063 (2007). The constitution establishes a framework for a prime minister as the chief executive, a bicameral parliament, and seven provinces. The Constituent Assembly, which had been charged under the interim constitution with bringing Nepal a constitution, transformed into the country's parliament upon the promulgation of the constitution. In November 2013 the country held national elections for the Constituent Assembly, which domestic and international observers characterized as credible, free, and fair.

Civilian authorities maintained effective control of security forces.

The most significant human rights problems included the alleged use of excessive force by security personnel in controlling protests, especially in the Terai region, that began in August 2015 in connection with the adoption of the constitution and did not end until February 2016. The government's failure for much of the year to initiate formal investigations into instances of alleged use of excessive force during the unrest was another source of concern. The government's delay in implementing and providing adequate resources for the country's two transitional justice mechanisms, the Truth and Reconciliation Commission (TRC) and the Commission on the Investigation of Enforced Disappeared Persons (CIEDP), as well as the lack of prosecutions for conflict-era crimes, reinforced the need for justice and accountability for human rights and humanitarian law violations during the country's 10-year insurgency (1996-2006). The constitution contains provisions that discriminate by gender, and discrimination against women and girls was a persistent problem.

Other human rights problems included poor prison and detention center conditions and police mistreatment of detainees. The courts remained vulnerable to political pressure, bribery, and intimidation. There were problems of harassment of media and press self-censorship. The government sometimes restricted freedom of assembly, notably in areas where violent protests against the constitutional process were taking place. The government limited freedoms for refugees, particularly for resident Tibetans. Corruption remained a problem at all levels of government. Citizenship laws and regulations that discriminate by gender contributed to statelessness. Early and forced marriage, and rape and domestic violence against women, including dowry-related deaths, remained serious problems. Violence against children, including reported abuse at orphanages, continued and rarely was prosecuted. Sex trafficking of adults and minors remained a significant problem. Discrimination against persons with disabilities, lower-caste individuals, and some ethnic groups continued, as did some harassment against gender and sexual minorities. There were some restrictions on worker rights. The government made little progress in combatting forced and bonded labor, which persisted despite laws banning the practice, and there was moderate progress in efforts to eliminate child labor.

The government routinely investigated and held accountable those officials and security forces accused of committing ongoing violations of the law. An exception to accountability was allegations of use of excessive force against protesters during the constitution-related unrest that took place from August 2015 through early February. In August the government approved the formation of an independent judicial commission to investigate alleged human rights violations during the constitutional unrest, but as of September, the commission had not started its work.

Section 1. Respect for the Integrity of the Person, Including Freedom from:

a. Arbitrary Deprivation of Life and other Unlawful or Politically Motivated Killings

There were several reports that the government or its agents committed arbitrary or unlawful killings. Civil unrest related to the promulgation of the constitution in September 2015, including protests, vandalism, and forced general strikes, in the mid-western hills and the Terai region continued into February. According to the National Human Rights Commission (NHRC), the Nepal Police and Armed Police Force (APF) killed 55 individuals, the majority of them protesters. While the majority of the deaths occurred in the early days of the protests in August and September 2015, three protesters were killed in 2016. Investigations by the NHRC, an independent constitutional body, and civil society, including Amnesty International, found the force used by security forces was excessive, disproportionate, or unnecessary. Some human rights groups and the NHRC claimed that police personnel carrying out crowd control activities failed to follow guidelines for escalating use of force set out in the Local Administration Act. According to the Act, security forces must aim below the knee when shooting at suspected criminals unless there is an imminent threat to human life. Police and some government officials claimed that the killings were justified because a large number of protesters presented an imminent threat to human life when they wielded sharp weapons, threw objects, set police vehicles and posts on fire, or otherwise directly attacked security personnel.

Media reported that police in Morang district killed three protesters in two separate incidents on January 21. According to the NGO Terai Human Rights Defenders Alliance (THRDA), Dropadi Devi Chaudhary and Mahadev Rishidev were killed in Rangeli municipality when police allegedly fired indiscriminately into a crowd that had gathered to protest the government of then Prime Minister Khadga Prasad Sharma Oli. THRDA reported that police shot Rishidev while he was fleeing the protest. In a separate incident the same day in Dainya Village Development Committee an APF officer allegedly fired into a crowd of protesters throwing rocks at a police van and killed Shivu Majhi. According to THRDA, the crowd was protesting police protection of hill-based youths who had earlier assaulted and harassed local Madhesi residents of Dainya.

For much of the year, the NHRC, local human rights activists, and international NGOs such as Human Rights Watch called for the creation of an independent investigation into the deaths and injuries that occurred during the political unrest. They accused the government of investigating attacks on police but refusing in many cases to register First Incident Reports on behalf of civilian victims. In August the government approved the formation of a judicial commission to investigate alleged human rights violations that occurred in the Terai. Also in August the government approved the payment of one million Nepali rupees (NRs) ($10,000) to each of the families of 52 persons (11 police and 41 protesters) killed during the unrest.

There were developments in a few emblematic conflict-era cases. In January the Supreme Court ruled against the government's 2011 pardon of Bal Krishna Dhungel, a Maoist politician convicted of killing Ujjan Kumar Shrestha in 1998. Despite the Supreme Court decision and order for his apprehension, Dhungel remained free, and was observed attending social functions during the year. Also in January the district court in Kavre reopened the case of Maina Sunar, who was allegedly tortured to death during the Maoist insurgency. The case had been put on hold in 2013 after the defendants, four former Nepal Army officers, failed to appear in court.

b. Disappearance

There were accusations of government involvement in a disappearance during the year. According to NGO Informal Sector Service Center (INSEC), local residents of Tatopani, Sindhupalchowk district reported that in March the APF arrested Kumar Tamang, a laborer temporarily living in Tatopani. Tamang's relatives, who were told by the local APF authorities they had not detained Tamang, staged a protest demanding an investigation into his whereabouts. Police initiated an investigation in March.

The fate of most of those who disappeared during the 1996-2006 civil conflict remained unknown. According to the NHRC, there were approximately 842 unresolved cases of disappearances, 594 of which may have involved state actors. As of December the government did not prosecute any government officials, current or former, for involvement in conflict-era disappearances, nor had it released information on the whereabouts of the 606 persons the NHRC identified as having been disappeared by state actors. The NHRC reported that Maoists were believed to be involved in 149 unresolved disappearances during the conflict. As of December, the government had not prosecuted any Maoists for involvement in disappearances. From April to August, CIEDP registered complaints from conflict-era victims, after which it commenced investigations into the complaints.

The overall number of conflict-era missing persons generally remained stable. As of August the International Committee of the Red Cross (ICRC) listed 1,334 names of missing persons, compared with 1,343 the previous year. The ICRC reported that, from January to August, two new cases were filed and six were closed. The CIEDP, however, registered 2,793 names during its complaint registration window.

c. Torture and Other Cruel, Inhuman, or Degrading Treatment or Punishment

Contrary to requirements in both the Interim Constitution of 2007 and the 2015 constitution, torture is not explicitly criminalized, and the law does not have clear guidelines for punishing offenders. The Torture Compensation Act provides for compensation for victims of torture; the victim must file a complaint and pursue the case through the courts.

According to human rights activists and legal experts, police resorted to severe abuse, primarily beatings, to force confessions. Based on interviews conducted with detainees, THRDA reported a slight increase in the rate of abuse from 2015. THRDA stated there had been no change to police abuse trends in rural parts of the Terai region and accused police of mistreating some individuals arrested in connection with the August 2015-February 2016 civil unrest in the Terai region. An Amnesty International report published in July accused police of subjecting members of the ethnic Tharu community in Kailali district to arbitrary arrest, torture, and other ill-treatment, and coercing some into signing forced confessions following the killing by protesters of eight security personnel and a child in Tikapur in August 2015.

THRDA stated that torture victims often were hesitant to file complaints due to police or other official intimidation and fear of retribution. According to THRDA, the courts ultimately dismissed many cases of alleged torture due to a lack of credible supporting evidence, especially medical documentation. In cases where courts awarded compensation or ordered disciplinary action against the police, the decisions rarely were implemented, according to THRDA and other NGOs.

THRDA reported that as of August, it had lodged several complaints of police abuse with the district courts, each of which remained pending. Separately, Advocacy Forum (AF) reported that as of August, it had filed nine torture compensation claims with district courts, all of which were ongoing. AF reported it did not file any cases with the Nepal Police Human Rights Commission (HRC), which has not responded to any of the 100 cases filed by AF since 2010. As of August the Nepal Police HRC reported receiving three complaints of torture, a decrease from last year's eight complaints, and two complaints of other cruel, inhuman, or degrading treatment. In the three cases alleging torture, 10 police personnel were found guilty and subject to departmental action, including demotion or hold of promotion and a note of official reprimand in their files. In the two cases alleging cruel treatment, two police personnel were subjected to administrative penalties.

According to AF's 2015 report on torture, 17.2 percent of the 1,212 detainees AF interviewed in 2015 were subjected to some form of physical abuse, compared with 16.2 percent in 2014. The same study indicated a slightly higher rate of reported torture among detainees identified as "indigenous." According to the Nepal Police HRC, the vast majority of the alleged incidents were not formally reported or investigated. Through August, the Nepal Police HRC inspected seven detention facilities in four districts and interviewed detainees about their treatment while in custody.

There have been no cases brought to the criminal justice system of torture committed during the civil conflict.

In February, the United Nations reported one allegation of sexual exploitation and abuse in South Sudan against a Nepalese peacekeeper for an incident that reportedly involved three adult victims. The peacekeeper was accused of sexual assault and transactional sex. The government continues to investigate the allegation.

Prison and Detention Center Conditions

Prison conditions, especially those in pretrial detention centers, were poor and did not meet international standards, according to human rights groups.

Physical Conditions: As of August there was overcrowding in the prison system, with 19,078 convicted prisoners in 74 prisons designed to hold 10,978 individuals. THRDA stated that overcrowding remained a serious problem in detention centers but noted some improvement as police opened new centers. Prison overcrowding was most severe in Banke District Prison, which incarcerated 643 inmates (an increase of 77 inmates compared with the previous year) in a facility designed to hold 150 individuals. A 2015 monitoring report by the Office of the Attorney General (OAG) indicated that eight prisons had more than twice as many inmates as their respective capacities. Due to overcrowding, according to the OAG report, there was not enough daylight or air due to an insufficient number of windows in one prison and four detention centers.

Authorities generally held pretrial detainees separately from convicted prisoners. Due to a lack of adequate juvenile detention facilities, authorities sometimes incarcerated pretrial detainee children with adults or allowed children to remain in jails with their incarcerated parents.

The OAG report indicated that the 27 detention centers the OAG monitored lacked separate facilities for women while the 12 prisons the OAG monitored had separate rooms for women.

According to the OAG report, six detention centers had no windows and four had no attached toilets or bathrooms. According to AF and THRDA, which monitor detention center conditions, medical examinations generally were perfunctory. AF also reported medical care was poor for detainees with serious conditions. The OAG report stated that kitchen facilities were either insufficient or lacking in three prisons. The OAG also reported that in one prison in Gulmi district and another in Mahottari district, some inmates slept on the floor due to lack of beds. According to AF, some detainees had access only to unfiltered and dirty water and inadequate food, and many detention centers had poor ventilation, lighting, heating, and bedding.

According to the NGO Child Workers in Nepal, minors housed in adult facilities often faced bullying from adult detainees and received poor treatment by police. Hygiene was poor, and police and adult detainees often made minors clean the toilets.

Administration: Recordkeeping in detention centers was poor, and falsification of arrest records was common, according to AF and THRDA. There were no alternatives to imprisonment or fines, or both, for nonviolent offenders.

An NHRC monitoring report stated that prison and detention facilities allowed prisoners to submit complaints through established procedures. AF, however, stated that detainees rarely made complaints due to threats and intimidation. Authorities were quicker to respond to allegations brought to their attention by NGOs or international organizations. There were no prison ombudsmen to handle prisoner complaints.

Independent Monitoring: There was no official institutional mechanism to monitor prisons or detention centers. The government generally allowed prison and pretrial detention center visits by the OAG, NHRC, the National Women's Commission, and the National Dalit Commission, as well as by lawyers of the accused. AF reported that some independent human rights observers, including the United Nations Office of the High Commissioner for Human Rights and ICRC, were given access to visit and monitor detention facilities but that on occasion some NGOs, including AF, were prevented from meeting with detainees or from accessing detention facilities. Media had no access to prisons or detention centers. The NHRC could request government action, but such requests often were denied.

Improvements: To address overcrowding in prisons, the government completed the construction of new prison facilities in Kaski, Nawalparasi, and Dang districts, but as of August only the Dang facility was in operation. The government also expanded the capacity of Nakhu prison from 250 to 700.

Although local NGOs did not cite major improvements in prison and detention center conditions, the Supreme Court ordered the government in August to increase food and allowances provided to prisoners. The government had been providing 700 grams of rice and 45 NRs (45 cents) per day to each prisoner. As of September the government had not complied with the order. Additionally, after inspecting the Khotang district prison in August and determining that landslides had damaged prison infrastructure and placed prisoners in danger, the NHRC requested the government to transfer 108 prisoners and five dependent children to a different facility. As of October 4, the government had not transferred the prisoners.

d. Arbitrary Arrest or Detention

The law prohibits arbitrary arrest and detention, but there were reports that security forces arbitrarily arrested persons during the year, particularly during widespread protests and political unrest in the Terai region from August 2015 to February 2016. Apart from the arbitrary arrests related to the political unrest, arbitrary arrests declined during the year, according to INSEC. The law gives chief district officers wide latitude to make arrests, and human rights groups contended that police abused their 24-hour detention authority by holding persons unlawfully, in some cases without proper access to counsel, food, and medicine, or in inadequate facilities.

As of August the Nepal Police HRC reported it had not received any complaints of arbitrary arrest or detention during the year, but on July 6, police in Kathmandu detained approximately 30 Tibetans during a celebration of the Dalai Lama's 81st birthday. They were released without charge several hours later.

Role of the Police and Security Apparatus

The Nepal Police is responsible for enforcing law and order across the country, while the APF is responsible for combating terrorism, providing security during riots and public disturbances, assisting in natural disasters, and protecting vital infrastructure, public officials, and the borders. In July 2015 the government gave the APF the authority to issue warrants to suspects they detain before turning them over to the Nepal Police. Generally, the Nepal Police and the APF execute search and arrest warrants without any prosecutorial or judicial review.

The Nepal Police, APF, and Nepal Army have human rights commissions (HRCs). The Nepal Army and Nepal Police HRCs have independent investigative powers. The Nepal Army's investigations were not fully transparent, according to human rights NGOs. Nepal Army HRC representatives stated that nearly all of its cases derived from the Maoist insurgency, and that full transparency could come only in the context of a functioning TRC. The Nepal Police also stated that conflict-era allegations of abuse should be handled in the context of a functioning TRC. From July 2015 to July 2016, the Nepal Police HRC reported three complaints, all of which related to allegations of torture and resulted in the punishment of 10 police officers. Seven officers received official reprimands and three were denied promotion. Additionally, for three pending torture cases from the previous fiscal year, the Nepal Police reprimanded five officers and gave another officer a warning letter. The Nepal Army HRC stated it received no complaints of human rights violations during the year. All security forces received human rights training prior to deployments on UN peacekeeping operations. The Nepal Police, APF, and Nepal Army HRCs provided human rights training to each individual in his respective organization. The APF and Nepal Police HRCs issued booklets outlining human rights best practices to nearly every police officer. The Nepal Army designates one officer in each brigade as a human rights officer.

Police corruption, especially among low-level and underpaid police officers, and lack of punishment for police abuses, remained problems.

Arrest Procedures and Treatment of Detainees

The law stipulates that, except in cases involving suspected security and narcotics violations, or when the crime's punishment would be more than three years' imprisonment, authorities must obtain an arrest warrant and present the suspect to a court within 24 hours of arrest (not including travel time). THRDA reported that among the cases of alleged torture it documented in 2016, none of the victims received a warrant at the time of arrest.

If the court upholds a detention, the law generally authorizes police to hold the suspect for up to 25 days to complete an investigation. In special cases (such as for suspected acts of corruption), a suspect can be held for up to six months. The constitution provides for access to a state-appointed lawyer or one of the detainee's choice, even if charges have not been filed. Few detainees could afford their own lawyer, and the justice system does not receive sufficient funding to provide free and competent counsel to indigent defendants.

Detainees have the legal right to receive visits by family members, but family access to prisoners varied from prison to prison. Defense attorneys were routinely denied access to defendants in custody. There is a system of bail, but bonds were too expensive for most citizens. The accused have the option of posting bail in cash or mortgaging their property to the court. Unless prisoners are released on recognizance (no bail), there are no alternatives to the bail system to ensure a defendant's appearance in court.

<u>Pretrial Detention</u>: Time served is credited to a prisoner's sentence, but pretrial detention occasionally exceeded the length of the ultimate sentence following trial and conviction.

Under the Public Security Act, security forces may detain persons who allegedly threaten domestic security and tranquility, amicable relations with other countries, or relations between citizens of different castes or religious groups. The government may detain persons in preventive detention for as long as 12 months without charging them with a crime, as long as the detention complies with the act's requirements. The court does not have any substantive legal role in preventive detentions under the act.

Other laws, including the Public Offenses Act, permit detention without charge for as long as 25 days with extensions. This act covers crimes such as disturbing the peace, vandalism, rioting, and fighting. Human rights monitors expressed concern that the act vests too much discretionary power in the chief district officer.

According to human rights groups, in some cases detainees appeared before judicial authorities well after the legally mandated 24-hour limit, allegedly to allow injuries from police mistreatment to heal. AF estimated in a 2015 report that 41 percent of detainees did not appear before judicial authorities within 24 hours of their arrests. THRDA stated police frequently circumvented the 24-hour requirement by registering the detainee's name only when they were ready to produce the detainee before the court.

<u>Detainee's Ability to Challenge Lawfulness of Detention before a Court</u>: Those arrested or detained are entitled to challenge in court the legal basis or arbitrary nature of their detention through *habeas corpus*. According to human rights lawyers, however, there were no cases of an individual receiving compensation for an illegal or arbitrary arrest or detention.

e. Denial of Fair Public Trial

The law provides for an independent judiciary, but courts remained vulnerable to political pressure, bribery, and intimidation. The Supreme Court has the right to review the constitutionality of laws.

Authorities did not consistently respect and implement court orders, including Supreme Court decisions, particularly decisions referring to conflict-era cases as discussed above.

Trial Procedures

The law provides for the right to counsel, equal protection under the law, protection from double jeopardy, protection from retroactive application of the law, public trials, and the right to be present at one's own trial, but these rights were not always applied. Defendants enjoy the presumption of innocence, except in some cases, such as human trafficking and drug trafficking, where the burden of proof is on the defendant. Judges decide cases; there is no jury system. The law provides detainees the right to legal representation and a court-appointed lawyer, a government lawyer, or access to private attorneys. The government provided legal counsel to indigent detainees only upon request. Persons who are unaware of their rights, in particular lower-caste individuals and members of some ethnic groups, may thus be deprived of legal representation. Defense lawyers reported having insufficient time to prepare their defense. In January, the Supreme Court issued a directive that courts must provide free interpretation services to those who do not speak Nepali. Defense lawyers may cross-examine accusers. By law, defense lawyers are entitled to access to government-held evidence, but such access can be difficult to obtain. All lower-court decisions, including acquittals, are subject to appeal. The Supreme Court is the court of last resort.

Military courts adjudicate cases concerning military personnel under the military code, which provides military personnel the same basic rights as civilians. The Army Act requires that soldiers accused of rape or homicide be handed over to civilian authorities for prosecution. Under normal circumstances, the army prosecutes all other criminal cases raised against soldiers under the military justice system. Despite this, the army has told the government that it is willing to cooperate with the TRC and CIEDP and will not "hide" behind the Army Act. Military courts cannot try civilians for crimes, even if the crimes involve the military services; civilian courts handle these cases.

Political Prisoners and Detainees

The government charged 58 civilians in connection with the killing of eight security personnel and a child during protests in Tikapur, Kailali district, in August 2015. According to THRDA, several of the 23 who were arrested were targeted because they were leaders and activists of the ethnic Tharu community, including Laxman Tharu, Dhaniram Chaudhary, and Lahuram Chaudhary. THRDA alleges that Laxman Tharu was not in the district at the time of the protest, Lahuram Chaudhary was not at the protest, and Dhaniram Chaudhary was a peaceful participant in the protest. As of August the murder and robbery trials for each of the three were ongoing.

Civil Judicial Procedures and Remedies

Individuals or organizations could seek remedies for human rights violations in national courts.

Property Restitution

The Maoists and their affiliate organizations have returned some previously seized property, as required by the 2006 Comprehensive Peace Accord that ended the civil conflict, but kept other illegally seized lands and properties. According to a report published in August 2014 by the Carter Center, a significant number of conflict-era land disputes remained outstanding.

f. Arbitrary or Unlawful Interference with Privacy, Family, Home, or Correspondence

The law allows police to conduct searches and seizures without a warrant if there is probable cause to believe that a crime has been committed, in which case a search may be conducted as long as two or more persons of "good character" are present. If a police officer has reasonable cause to believe that a suspect may possess material evidence, the officer must submit a written request to another officer to conduct a search, and there must be another official present who holds at least the rank of assistant sub-inspector. Some legal experts claimed that by excluding prosecutors and judges from the warrant procedure, police have relatively few checks against their discretion.

The law prohibits arbitrary interference with privacy, family, home, and correspondence. The government generally respected these prohibitions.

Section 2. Respect for Civil Liberties, Including:

a. Freedom of Speech and Press

The constitution and the law provide for freedom of speech and press, and the government generally respected these rights. In some cases, the government failed to enforce the law effectively. Human rights lawyers and some journalists stated that the constitution expanded the ability of the government to restrict freedom of speech and press in ways they considered vague and open to abuse. In comparison with the interim constitution, the 2015 constitution sets out more circumstances under which laws curtailing freedom of speech and press may be formulated. These include acts that "jeopardize harmonious relations between federal units" and acts that assist a foreign state or organization to jeopardize national security. The constitution prohibits any acts "contrary to public health, decency, and morality" or that "disturb the public law and order situation." The same provision of the constitution also prohibits persons from converting other persons from one religion to another or disturbing the religion of others.

Freedom of Speech and Expression: Citizens generally believed they could voice their opinions freely and often expressed critical opinions in print and electronic media without restriction. In July the government limited freedom of expression for the members of Kathmandu's Tibetan community by interfering with a planned celebration of the Dalai Lama's birthday; however, the government allowed Tibetans to celebrate other events throughout the year.

On May 2, Robert Penner, a Canadian citizen, was arrested for posting messages to Twitter that expressed support for Madhesi protesters and criticism of the government's human rights record. Police ordered Penner to depart the country within two days for allegedly sowing "social disorder" and engaging in conduct against the "national interest," citing a provision of the immigration law. The Supreme Court decided against granting a stay order on Penner's deportation, saying there was no need as he had already departed the country.

Press and Media Freedoms: The independent media were active and expressed a wide variety of views without restriction, with a few exceptions. On May 23, police arrested Shesh Narayan Jha, a photographer and chief editor of *Sahayatra* (an online student publication) and managing editor of *Samayabodh* magazine, for taking photos of a protester who had smeared paint on the gate of Singha Durbar, the main government complex in Kathmandu. Initially charged under the Public Offense Act of 1970, Jha and the protester were later released.

Violence and Harassment: According to the Federation of Nepali Journalists (FNJ), the government did not make sufficient efforts to preserve the safety and independence of the media and rarely prosecuted individuals who attacked journalists, in particular those who were reporting on the Terai unrest. The FNJ also stated that some members of the security forces attempted to prevent the press from freely covering protests.

<u>Censorship or Content Restrictions</u>: The constitution prohibits prior censorship of material for printing, publication or broadcasting, including electronically. The constitution also provides that the government cannot revoke media licenses, close media houses, or seize material based on the content of what is printed, published, or broadcast. The constitution, however, also provides for "reasonable restrictions" on these rights for acts or incitement that "may undermine the sovereignty, territorial integrity, nationality of Nepal, or harmonious relations between the federal units or harmonious relations between the various castes, tribes, religions, or communities." Speech amounting to treason, defamation, or contempt of court is also prohibited.

Media professionals expressed concern about an additional provision in the constitution that allows the government to formulate laws to regulate media. Such laws could be used to close down media houses or cancel their registration. The constitution also includes publication and dissemination of false materials as grounds for imposing legal restrictions on press freedom.

Although by law all media outlets, including government-owned stations, operated independently from direct government control, indirect political influence sometimes led to self-censorship. This was particularly true of stories that could be considered politically provocative. The FNJ stated that journalists working for Terai-based media or for major national media in the Terai region exercised self-censorship during protests over the constitution.

Internet Freedom

The government did not restrict or disrupt access to the internet or censor online content, and there were no credible reports that the government monitored private online communications without appropriate legal authority. The Electronic Transaction Act of 2008 prohibits publication in electronic form of material that may be "contrary to the public morality or decent behavior," may "spread hate or jealousy," or may "jeopardize the harmonious relations subsisting among the peoples of various castes, tribes and communities." Authorities took action under the Electronic Transaction Act in an incident relating to material posted on social media. On May 8, police arrested Manoj Kumar Rai, also known as Bhadragol Kirati, chief editor of *Gaunle* magazine, after he published and posted on Facebook material that criticized Bhakta Bahadur Rai, a self-declared religious guru. Police held Rai in custody for 10 days before the court released him on bail.

On June 14, the government approved the Online Media Operation Directive, which requires all Nepal-based online news and opinion websites to be registered. The directive gives the government the authority to block websites based on content if that content lacks an "authoritative source," creates "a misconception," or negatively affects international relationships. The government also has the authority to block content that threatens the country's sovereignty, territorial integrity, nationality, or harmonious relations. Online sedition, defamation, contempt of court, or indecent and immoral content may also be blocked. Media experts and journalists expressed concern that the directive's vague language gives the government power to censor online content arbitrarily, threatening freedom of press and online freedom of expression. As a result of such criticism, the government formed a three-member panel to amend the directive. As of August no changes had been made to the directive.

Academic Freedom and Cultural Events

The law provides for the freedom to hold cultural events. Government permits are required to hold large public events. During the year the Tibetan community did not request permission for a number of small events confined to their settlements or within monasteries; they did not face repercussions although they faced restrictions (see section 2.b.). Authorities granted approval to the Tibetan community to organize a ceremony for the third day of the Tibetan New Year on February 11, but a celebration planned in Kathmandu for the Dalai Lama's birthday on July 6 was cut short due to police interference. With the exception of the Dalai Lama's birthday, Tibetans throughout the Kathmandu Valley attended such events with minimal reports of restrictions of movement.

b. Freedom of Peaceful Assembly and Association

The law provides for the freedoms of assembly and association; however, the government sometimes restricted freedom of assembly.

Freedom of Assembly

Freedom of assembly generally was respected for citizens and legal residents, but during the period of widespread civil unrest in the mid-western hills and Terai region, local officials imposed curfews and bans on gatherings in numerous districts and localities where violence had occurred. The law authorizes chief district officers to impose curfews when there is a possibility that demonstrations or riots could disturb the peace. The district administration offices in many Terai districts also declared certain zones to be "riot-affected areas." In such zones gatherings of five or more persons were prohibited (under "prohibitory orders") and police could arrest and search individuals without warrants. Such declarations also empowered chief district officers to call in the army to assist civilian security forces, a situation that occurred in some districts. Human rights organizations accused police of using excessive force, including firing rubber bullets and live ammunition, to enforce curfews and prohibitory orders, in some cases leading to deaths and injuries.

Freedom of Association

The law provides for freedom of association, and the government generally respected this right.

c. Freedom of Religion

See the Department of State's *International Religious Freedom Report* at www.state.gov/religiousfreedomreport/.

d. Freedom of Movement, Internally Displaced Persons, Protection of Refugees, and Stateless Persons

The law provides for freedom of internal movement, foreign travel, emigration, and repatriation, except for most refugees, whose freedom of movement within the country is legally limited. Constraints on refugee movements were enforced unevenly. The government cooperated with the Office of the UN High Commissioner for Refugees (UNHCR) and other humanitarian organizations in providing protection and assistance to refugees and asylum seekers.

Some political groups attempted to restrict freedom of movement, including through forced general strikes known locally as "bandhs," to pressure the government and civil society. General strikes from August 2015 through February 2016 enforced by Madhesi parties, the National Federation of Indigenous Nationalities, the Rastriya Prajatantra Party-Nepal, and other groups severely restricted mobility, supply of fuel, daily goods, and access to services for an extended period. In some instances protesters and alleged criminal operatives attacked civilians believed to be defying the general strike or opposing their cause, leading to at least two civilian deaths.

<u>Abuse of Migrants, Refugees, and Stateless Persons</u>: Police reportedly conducted checks of identity documents of Tibetans, including monks and nuns, at checkpoints. During the celebration of the Dalai Lama's birthday on July 6, police detained 30 Tibetans, releasing them without charge later the same day.

<u>In-country Movement</u>: The government has not issued personal identification documents to Tibetan refugees in more than 20 years, leaving the majority of this refugee population without recourse to present required documents at police checkpoints or during police stops. Some refugees reported being harassed or turned around by police at checkpoints.

<u>Foreign Travel</u>: In an attempt to protect women from being trafficked or abused, the government maintained a minimum age of 24 (lowered from 30 in May) for women traveling overseas for domestic employment. NGOs and human rights activists viewed the age ban as discriminatory and counterproductive because it impelled some women to migrate through informal channels across the Indian border.

Internally Displaced Persons

The April 2015 earthquake and its aftershocks caused widespread devastation and displaced millions of individuals, particularly in the 14 most-affected districts. According to the International Organization for Migration, as of August, 65 active sites were hosting 18,292 individuals in 11 districts, including 2,108 children under age five.

It remains unclear what proportion of this population is unable or unwilling to return to their homes. Many remain in the camps because they do not hold a title to land and were squatting when the earthquake occurred. Others stay because their homes remain vulnerable to or were destroyed by subsequent landslides. The National Reconstruction Authority has not finalized a policy on how to address the reconstruction needs of this displaced population. In some locations, the government began building structures that will house multiple families, to serve as a medium-term solution for earthquake-displaced populations. Humanitarian agencies have concerns that housing multiple families in the same unit could exacerbate many challenges faced by internally displaced persons (IDPs), particularly a lack of privacy and security for women and girls; insufficient access to toilets and bathing and changing areas; complicated family sleeping arrangements; and difficulties dealing with menstruation and pregnancy. Other common challenges faced by IDPs included insufficient protection from the weather, limited access to water and food, emotional stress, and elevated vulnerability to trafficking.

Although the government and the Maoists agreed to support the voluntary return in safety and dignity of IDPs to their homes following the 10-year civil war, the agreement has not been fully implemented. The Ministry of Peace and Reconstruction estimated that 78,700 persons were displaced from 1996 to 2006, but an estimated 50,000 were unwilling or unable to return home. The reasons included unresolved land and property issues, lack of citizenship or ownership documentation, and security concerns since the land taken from IDPs by Maoists during the conflict was often sold or given to landless or tenant farmers.

The government provided relief packages for the rehabilitation and voluntary return of conflict-era IDPs. Many of those still displaced preferred to integrate locally and live in urban areas, mostly as illegal occupants of government land along riversides or together with the landless population. The absence of public services and lack of livelihood assistance also impeded the return of IDPs.

Protection of Refugees

Access to Asylum: The laws do not provide for the determination of individual refugee or asylum claims or a comprehensive legal framework for refugee protection. The government recognized large numbers of Bhutanese and Tibetans as refugees and supported resettlement of Bhutanese refugees to foreign countries. The government does not provide for local integration as a durable solution.

The government officially restricted freedom of movement and work for the approximately 15,000 Bhutanese refugees residing in the two remaining refugee camps in the eastern part of the country, but those restrictions were largely unenforced for this population. The government officially does not allow Bhutanese refugees to work or have access to public education or public health clinics, but it allows UNHCR to provide parallel free education and health services to refugees in the camps. In 2007 the government agreed to permit third-country resettlement for Bhutanese refugees. Since resettlement began, more than 104,000 Bhutanese refugees have been resettled in foreign countries.

The government does not recognize Tibetans who arrived in the country after 1989 as refugees. Most Tibetans who arrived since then transited to India, although an unknown number remained in the country. The government has not issued refugee cards to Tibetan refugees since 1995. UNHCR estimated more than half of the

15,000 to 20,000 resident Tibetan refugees remained undocumented. After China heightened security along its border and increased restrictions on internal freedom of movement for ethnic Tibetans in 2008, the number of Tibetans who transited through the country dropped significantly. UNHCR reported that 89 Tibetans transited the country in 2015, and 44 from January through June in 2016. The government issued UNHCR-facilitated exit permits for recent arrivals from Tibet who were transiting en route to India.

Access to Basic Services: Most Tibetan refugees who lived in the country, particularly those who arrived after 1990 or turned 16 after 1995, did not have documentation, nor did their Nepal-born children. Even those with acknowledged refugee status had no legal rights beyond the ability to remain in the country. The Nepal-born children of Tibetans with legal status often lacked documentation. The government allowed NGOs to provide primary- and secondary-level schooling to Tibetans living in the country. Tibetan refugees had no entitlement to higher education in public or private institutions and were denied the right to work officially. They were unable legally to obtain business licenses, driver's licenses, or bank accounts, or to own property, or consistently document births, marriages, and deaths. Some in the Tibetan community resorted to bribery to obtain these services. While Nepal-based Tibetans with refugee certificates were eligible to apply for travel documents to leave the country, the legal process was often arduous, expensive, and opaque. In April the government issued a directive authorizing chief district officers to skip the verification step, which required witnesses and a police letter, for Tibetans who had previously been issued a travel document.

More than 500 refugees and asylum seekers from other countries, including Pakistan, Burma, Afghanistan, Sri Lanka, Bangladesh, Somalia, Iran, Iraq, and Democratic Republic of the Congo, lived in the country. The government continued to deny these groups recognition as refugees, even when recognized as such by UNHCR, and required prohibitive fines--$5 per day out of status--and a discretionary penalty of up to NRs 50,000 (about $500) to obtain an exit permit. The government did not waive fines nor change its policy to enable other registered refugees destined for resettlement or repatriation to obtain exit permits without paying these fines. The government allowed UNHCR to provide some education, health, and livelihood services to these refugees, but the refugees lacked legal access to public education and the right to work.

Stateless Persons

An estimated 5.2 million individuals--23 percent of the population age 16 and over--lacked citizenship documentation. Citizenship documents, which are issued at age 16, are required to register to vote, register marriages or births, buy or sell land, appear in professional exams, open bank accounts or gain access to credit, and receive state social benefits. Prior to the 2013 constituent assembly election, the government deployed citizenship/voter registration mobile teams to remote areas to issue citizenship cards and register new voters. The Home Ministry reported issuing more than 600,000 new citizenship cards during the exercise.

Constitutional provisions, laws, and regulations governing citizenship discriminated by gender, contributing to statelessness. The constitution states that citizenship is derived from one Nepali parent, but it also stipulates that a child born to a Nepali mother and a non-Nepali father may obtain citizenship only through naturalization. Securing citizenship papers for the child of Nepali parents, even when the mother possessed Nepali citizenship documents, was extremely difficult, except in cases in which the child's father supported the application. These difficulties persisted despite a 2011 Supreme Court decision granting a child Nepali citizenship through the mother if the father was unknown or absent.

The constitution states that the children of unidentified fathers may obtain citizenship through their mothers, but if it is later determined that the father is a foreign citizen, the child will lose citizenship by descent and be eligible for naturalization. According to human rights lawyers, this provision could apply to the children of single mothers, including rape and trafficking victims, but would not address situations in which the father was known but refused to acknowledge paternity. The legal and practical restrictions on transferring citizenship imposed particular hardships on children whose fathers were deceased, had abandoned the family, or (as was increasingly common) departed the country to work abroad. Since naturalization is not a fundamental right under the constitution, although it could be an option for those not eligible for citizenship by descent, it is subject to state discretion. Human rights lawyers reported that the government has not processed any such applications for naturalization of children in recent years.

For women and girls to obtain citizenship by descent for themselves, regulations require a married woman to submit a formal attestation from her husband, father, or her husband's family (if widowed) that she qualifies for citizenship and has his or their permission to receive it, thereby making a woman's right to citizenship contingent on her father's or husband's cooperation. In many cases, husbands refused to provide their wives this attestation. Preventing women from obtaining citizenship documentation precludes their access to the courts and thus their ability to make legal claims to land and other property, leaving the husband or male relatives free to stake their own claims.

While stateless persons did not experience violence, they experienced discrimination in employment, education, housing, health services, marriage, birth registration, identity documentation, access to courts and judicial procedures, migration opportunities, land and property ownership, and access to earthquake relief and reconstruction programs.

Section 3. Freedom to Participate in the Political Process

The law provides citizens the ability to choose their government in free and fair periodic elections held by secret ballot and based on universal and equal suffrage.

Elections and Political Participation

Recent Elections: In November 2013 citizens participated in the country's second Constituent Assembly elections, which international and domestic observers deemed essentially credible, free, and fair. In an effort to obstruct the 2013 elections, a breakaway Maoist faction, the Communist Party of Nepal-Maoist, committed acts of political violence and intimidation and attempted to enforce a 10-day transportation ban. Despite such efforts, the Election Commission reported that more than 74 percent of registered voters participated, the highest figure in the country's history. According to domestic and international observers, including the Carter Center and the EU, the elections were conducted well and generally were free of major irregularities.

There have not been local elections since 1997. Elected local councils were dissolved in 2002; in their absence, senior civil servants have conducted local administration in consultation with local political party representatives who do not necessarily have any tie to the region for which they have responsibility.

Participation of Women and Minorities: No specific laws restrict women or minorities from voting, running for office, serving as electoral monitors, or otherwise participating in government or political parties. The constitution mandates that at least one third of all members of the lower house of the federal parliament must be women and requires inclusion of various minority groups in the list of candidates in the 40 percent of seats chosen through a proportional representation system. The constitution also stipulates that in the upper house of the federal parliament, for the 56 members chosen by an electoral college, the eight members from each of the seven provinces must include at least three women, one member of the Dalit caste, and one person with a disability or member of a minority group. Additionally, of the remaining three members of the upper house chosen by the president, at least one must be a woman.

Tradition and relative socioeconomic disadvantage limited the participation of women, some castes, and some ethnic groups in the political process, including as elected officials. The larger political parties had associated women's wings, youth wings, trade unions, and social organizations. Women, youth, and minorities complained that party leaders, mostly upper-caste men from the central hills, prohibited meaningful political participation despite the existence of certain quotas for participation.

Section 4. Corruption and Lack of Transparency in Government

Although the law provides criminal penalties for corruption by officials, there continued to be reports that officials engaged in corrupt practices with impunity.

Corruption: In February the Commission for the Investigation of the Abuse of Authority (CIAA), filed a graft case against Inspector General of the Armed Police Force Kosh Raj Onta. Onta, along with eight other APF officers, allegedly embezzled 68 million NRs (about $680,000) in a false invoicing scheme. The CIAA also filed graft cases against 36 officials of the Poverty Alleviation Fund, a government body, for allegedly embezzling NRs 43 million ($430,000) over the course of three years.

The CIAA took Sajha Yatayat (Public Transit) Chairman Kanak Mani Dixit into custody on April 22 for his alleged involvement in public corruption. Dixit, who is also a senior journalist and co-publisher of *Himalmedia,* has a history of criticizing CIAA Chief Commissioner Lokman Singh Karki. According to the CIAA, Dixit was taken into custody for amassing property valued at an amount disproportionate to his known source of income. Dixit and his supporters alleged that the CIAA action was an act of revenge for Dixit's public opposition to Karki's appointment as CIAA Chief Commissioner. In May the Supreme Court ordered Dixit's release but allowed the investigation into his alleged financial irregularities to continue. Media and activists have accused CIAA Chief Commissioner Karki of pursuing investigations beyond the jurisdiction of the CIAA, selectively prosecuting political enemies, and misusing public funds and facilities.

There were numerous reports of corrupt actions by government officials, political parties, and party-affiliated organizations. As in previous years, student and labor groups associated with political parties demanded contributions from schools and businesses. Corruption and impunity remained general problems within the Nepal Police and Armed Police Force.

Financial Disclosure: Public officials are subject to financial disclosure laws. According to the National Vigilance Center, the body mandated to monitor financial disclosures and make them available to the public, in fiscal year 2014-2015, 22,860 civil servants did not submit their annual financial statements as required by law. Public officials may face a fine of up to NRs 5,000 ($50). The CIAA publicly demanded that officials be more diligent in submitting financial disclosure reports. Ministers are required to submit their property details within two months of assuming office. During the period covered by the latest National Vigilance Center report, July 2014 to July 2015, 22 of the 23 ministers in office did so. Despite the CIAA requirement that officials submit information regarding their property holdings, CIAA Chief Commissioner Karki has been accused of failing to do so since he assumed office in 2014. According to press reports, 55 citizens filed a case with the CIAA under the Right to Information Act demanding the release of Karki's property disclosure information. When the CIAA failed to release the information, the requestors filed a case with the National Information Commission, which adjudicates cases in which petitioners allege wrongful denial of access to information.

Public Access to Information: The constitution provides for the right to information on any matters of concern to oneself or the public, but it does not compel the government to provide information protected by law. The government's National Information Commission, formed pursuant to the 2007 Right to Information Act, is charged with adjudicating cases in which petitioners allege they have been wrongly denied access to information, that information has been improperly classified, or that individuals were punished for whistle-blowing. The act also provides for punitive measures in cases of defiance. The commission, which responds to complaints within 45 days and to appeals within 60 days, received 678 cases from July 2015 to July 2016, the country's fiscal year.

Section 5. Governmental Attitude Regarding International and Nongovernmental Investigation of Alleged Violations of Human Rights

While domestic and international human rights groups generally were free to operate, investigate, and publish their findings on human rights cases, the government placed administrative burdens on some international NGOs by complicating procedures for obtaining visas and compelling them to sign asset control documents.

<u>Government Human Rights Bodies</u>: The NHRC investigated allegations of abuses, but resource constraints, insufficient staff (232 out of 309 positions were vacant as of August), and limitations on its mandate led some activists to view the body as ineffective and insufficiently independent. The NHRC claimed the government helped promote impunity by failing to implement its recommendations fully. The NHRC stated in its most recent report that from its establishment in 2000 through 2013, it had made recommendations for prosecution and reparations in 738 cases regarding 1,577 victims. More than three-quarters of these involved conflict-era incidents. The NHRC noted the government had fully implemented 14 percent of these recommendations by carrying out prosecution and awarding reparations, and partially implemented 48 percent through reparations alone. In the remaining cases, the government did not implement the NHRC's recommendations for prosecution or reparations.

In April the then prime minister summoned the NHRC chair and other commissioners to question them about a statement delivered in Geneva by NHRC Commissioner Mohna Ansari during the Universal Periodic Review of the human rights situation in the country. In her March address to the UN Human Rights Council, Ansari raised concerns about discriminatory citizenship provisions in the constitution, the government's failure to investigate killings and the excessive use of force during political unrest in the Terai, and the need for a credible transitional justice process. Amnesty International, Human Rights Watch, the International Commission of Jurists, and local human rights activists criticized the government for intimidation and harassment of the NHRC.

The government and judiciary did not significantly address conflict-era human rights and humanitarian law violations committed by the Nepal Army, Nepal Police, APF, and Maoist parties. Human rights advocates expressed concern that several *sub judice* cases of conflict-era abuses by such actors before criminal courts would be removed from judicial jurisdiction and inappropriately "transferred" to the TRC or CIEDP. In this scenario, the TRC or CIEDP would review the cases as it would with any other registered complaint and decide whether to recommend prosecution.

The TRC and CIEDP began their two-year terms, which are extendable by one year, in February 2015. During their first year, they carried out a series of preparatory tasks, including drafting regulations for cabinet approval as well as codes of conduct and operating procedures; hiring staff and procuring equipment and facilities; and conducting consultations with victims and other stakeholders.

In April the TRC and CIEDP launched the first operational phase by registering conflict-era complaints from victims at their main offices in Kathmandu and district headquarter-based Local Peace Committees. Although the two commissions also accepted applications by phone, international monitoring organizations report that few victims were aware of the option. The complaint registration process was initially scheduled to last two months, but the commissions extended the deadline through August 10 under pressure from local victims' groups and international NGOs. Victims' groups and monitoring organizations criticized the commissions for a lack of outreach, failure to explain how they planned to use information provided by victims, and failure to recognize the difficulty many victims faced in traveling to district headquarters to register complaints. Other factors that have contributed to a lack of victim trust in the transitional justice process include accusations that the commissions have failed to protect victim confidentiality, reports of occasional interference and intimidation by security forces, a lack of gender sensitive procedures, and continued politicization by political parties. Through August 10, the TRC had registered 53,000 conflict-era complaints, and the CIEDP registered 2,793 cases.

Local human rights advocates cite a number of legal shortcomings that pose obstacles to a comprehensive and credible transitional justice process in the country. For example, the law does not criminalize torture or enforced disappearance, and the statute of limitations for rape is only 180 days. Additionally, the law does not specifically recognize war crimes or crimes against humanity, though the constitution recognizes as law treaties to which the country is a party. Critics also cite a number of instances in which the government has failed to implement Supreme Court decisions. For example, in a February 2015 ruling, the court nullified provisions of the TRC and CIEDP Act that would have granted the commissions discretionary power to recommend amnesty for serious crimes, stating that amnesty would violate the then-interim constitution and international obligations. The court also nullified provisions that could have required reconciliation between victims and perpetrators without the victims' consent. Additionally, the court struck down a provision that would have given the Ministry of Peace and Reconstruction the authority to vet TRC and CIEDP recommendations for prosecution, and ruled the two commissions could not supplant the normal justice system in prosecuting conflict-era crimes. As of

August, the government had not amended the acts to bring them in line with the Supreme Court decision.

Section 6. Discrimination, Societal Abuses, and Trafficking in Persons

Women

<u>Rape and Domestic Violence</u>: Violence against women and girls remained a problem. Under the civil code, prison sentences for rape vary between five and 15 years depending on the victim's age. The law also mandates five years' additional imprisonment in the case of gang rape, rape of pregnant women, or rape of a woman with disabilities. The victim's compensation depends on the degree of mental and physical abuse. The Bill to Amend Some Nepal Acts to Maintain Gender Equality and End Gender-Based Violence, which was signed into law in October 2015, increased the sentence for marital rape from three to six months' imprisonment to three to five years' imprisonment. The bill also extends the statute of limitations for filing rape charges from 35 days to 180 days. Despite its extension of the statute of limitations, human rights groups highlighted concerns with the act and its implications for addressing sexual violence committed during the country's 10-year conflict.

Many incidents of rape went unreported although NGOs stated that reporting has increased, in part due to improved awareness. For rape cases that were reported, police and the courts were responsive. According to NGOs, police frequently prioritized cases of sexual violence, and the District Court Regulations stipulates that judges should expedite cases of rape, human trafficking, and other violent crimes.

Rape, sexual violence, and other forms of victimization suffered disproportionately by women and girls during the country's 10-year conflict remained unresolved and unaddressed. Men and boys also were victims of rape and sexual assault during the conflict.

Domestic violence against women and girls remained a serious problem. There was much anecdotal evidence that physical and verbal abuse was common, with human rights organization INSEC reporting an increase in incidents of reported domestic violence during the year, in part due to increased awareness. Violence against women and girls was believed to be one of the major factors responsible for women's relative poor health, livelihood insecurity, and inadequate social mobilization. Additionally, NGOs reported that the practice of early and forced marriage, which remained prevalent, limited girls' access to education and increased their susceptibility to domestic violence and sexual abuse. The Domestic Violence (Crime and Punishment) Act of 2009 allows for settling complaints of domestic violence through mediation with an emphasis on reconciliation. Legal prosecution under the act was usually pursued only when mediation failed. The act's criminal provisions stipulate a fine of NRs 3,000 to 25,000 ($30 to $250), six months' imprisonment, or both, for violators. Repeat offenders receive double punishment. Any person holding a position of public responsibility is subject to 10 percent greater punishment than a person who does not hold such a position. Anyone who does not follow a court order is subject to a fine of NRs 2,000 to 15,000 ($20 to $150), four months' imprisonment, or both.

Reports from women's rights defenders suggested that the majority of incidents of domestic violence against women and girls were unreported, although reporting has increased, in part due to improved awareness. According to INSEC, although police conducted training on enforcement of the Domestic Violence Act, most reported incidents were resolved through mediation, and repeat violations after reconciliation by the same perpetrators were not uncommon. In addition, cases of severe domestic violence are sometimes filed under the Domestic Violence Act rather than as crimes with greater punishments, such as assault, battery, or attempted murder. Nonetheless, the Women's Rehabilitation Center (WOREC) stated that domestic violence cases were increasingly handled by women and children service centers (commonly known as women's cells) of the Nepal Police, and that in these instances the police were more responsive and treated the victims better. District women and children offices offered public education and psychosocial services and operated hotlines and shelters in 35 districts to address all forms of gender-based violence, including violence that affects child brides. According to the Ministry of Women, Children, and Social Welfare, although the government shelters welcome victims of child marriage into the shelters, the number of such victims seeking shelter and support is near zero.

NGOs offered educational programs for police, politicians, and the general public to promote greater awareness of domestic violence. The Nepal Police had women's cells staffed by female officers in each of the country's 75 districts to make it easier for women and girls to report crimes to the police. The number of women's cells and officers assigned to them increased substantially during the last three years. According to the Women and Children Service Directorate, many women's cells were not fully operational, but the Nepal Police, with outside assistance, endeavored to build and improve their infrastructure and capacity. NGOs stated that despite improvements, resources and training to deal with victims of domestic violence and trafficking were insufficient. Although police guidelines call on officers to treat domestic violence as a criminal offense, this was difficult to implement outside of the women's cells due to entrenched discriminatory attitudes. NGOs reported that girls, including those forced into early marriage, are less aware of their rights and are more susceptible to social pressure. As a result, they are less likely to file a complaint with the police or seek services from the government or NGOs.

The Office of the Prime Minister and Council of Ministers' 2011 standard operating procedure for prevention of and response to gender-based violence (GBV) has led to the establishment of service centers in 17 districts, rehabilitation centers in eight districts, and hospital-based one-stop crisis management centers in 17 districts to provide treatment, protection, and psychosocial and legal support for survivors of GBV. Gender experts say the standard operating procedure has led to improved coordination among police, NHRC, National Women's Commission, chief district officers, local authorities, community mediation centers, and NGOs working to address violence against women and girls. In remote areas, however, awareness of resources for women and girls and the ability of the government to enforce legislation governing GBV and child marriage remained low.

Although the law generally prohibits polygamy, there are exceptions if the wife is infertile, sick, or crippled. According to the latest Nepal Demographic Health Survey in 2011, 4 percent of women and 2 percent of men lived in polygamous unions. Polygamists not covered under the above exceptions are subject to a one- to two-year prison term and a fine, but the second marriage is not invalidated.

Other Harmful Traditional Practices: The constitution criminalizes violence against or oppression of women based on religious, social, or cultural traditions and gives victims the right to compensation. According to traditional practice, a bride's family must pay the husband's family a predetermined amount, or dowry, based on the husband's training and education. The practice of paying dowries is illegal, with penalties of up to NRs 10,000 ($100) and prison sentences of up to three years. Additionally, the 2015 Act to Amend Some Nepal Acts to Maintain Gender Equality and End Gender-Based Violence stipulates that any psychological abuse of women, including asking for dowry, humiliation, physical torture, and shunning women for not providing a dowry, is punishable. Nevertheless, dowries remained common, especially in the Terai region. Government agencies documented incidents of dowry-related violence, recommended interventions, and occasionally rescued victims and offered them rehabilitation services.

The law does not allow mediation of dowry-related violence. NGOs nevertheless stated that local communities often pressure victims not to file criminal complaints of dowry-related violence, or to withdraw complaints, and then facilitate mediation between the victim and perpetrator. Women's rights activists stated that the high cost of dowries significantly contributed to gender-based violence in much of the Terai region, where there were sporadic incidents of killing or attempted killing of brides over dowry disputes, despite efforts to eradicate the practice. Activists claimed that in Dhanusa district, for example, the cost of a dowry had increased over the past several years from the cost of a cow (NRs 25,000 or $250) to between NRs 400,000 and NRs two million ($4,000 to $20,000), demanded in cash. In some cases, as part of a pre-dowry agreement, the bride's family will pay the tuition fee for the bridegroom to pursue academic study. Activists reported that many men left the country to work abroad to earn money to pay for family members' dowries, which left the men's wives more vulnerable to abuse.

Traditional beliefs about witchcraft negatively affected rural women, especially widows, the elderly, persons of low economic status, or members of the Dalit caste. Shamans or family members publicly beat and otherwise physically abused alleged witches as part of exorcism ceremonies. Media and NGOs reported numerous cases of such violence, and civil society organizations raised public awareness of the problem. Women, and in some instances men, accused of witchcraft were severely traumatized and suffered physical and mental abuse, including being fed human excreta, being hit with hot spoons in different parts of the body, being forced to touch hot irons or breathe in chili smoke, having their genitals perforated, or being banished from their community. According to reports compiled by INSEC, 51 women accused of witchcraft were victims of violence in 2015, compared with 89 in 2014, with at least 12 victims in the first half of 2016. Government agencies recorded incidents of violence related to witchcraft allegations, recommended interventions, and occasionally rescued victims and offered them rehabilitation services; however, as with dowry-related violence, communities often forced victims into mediation with perpetrators in violation of the law.

The 2015 Anti-Witchcraft (Crime and Punishment) Act, the first legal mechanism to address directly such abuse, imposes prison sentences of five to 10 years and fines of up to NRs 100,000 ($1,000) for those who physically or mentally abuse women accused of being witches or men accused of sorcery. It also imposes prison sentences of up to five years for those who evict supposed witches or banish them from their communities. Information was unavailable on the number of individuals prosecuted under the act in 2016. INSEC stated that because the act was passed in August 2015, people remained confused about which law to cite in registering and prosecuting anti-witchcraft cases.

The practice of "chhaupadi" (expelling women and girls from their homes during menstruation and sometimes following childbirth, including forcing women and girls to reside in cattle sheds) continued to be a serious problem. Chhaupadi persists despite a 2005 Supreme Court decision outlawing the practice and guidelines on eliminating it issued in 2008 by the Ministry of Women, Children, and Social Welfare. The practice puts adolescent girls, women, and infants who are expelled with their mothers at risk of exposure to extreme elements, predators, and infection. The most recent Nepal Multi-Index Survey in 2010 reported that while 19 percent of women between the ages of 15 and 49 nationwide practiced chhaupadi, the problem was particularly acute in the hilly regions in the country's mid- and far-west, where approximately 50 percent of women followed the practice. Women in Kathmandu also reported being forced to practice a less extreme form of chhaupadi and generally were not allowed in the kitchen or any place where religious rituals were being practiced. Chhaupadi directly limited many girls' access to education for a large portion of the academic year.

Sexual Harassment: The 2014 Sexual Harassment at the Workplace (Elimination) Act allows the top administrative official in a district to impose up to six months' imprisonment, a maximum fine of NRs 50,000 ($500), or both, against a perpetrator, once a series of internal workplace processes to address a complaint have been exhausted. According to women's rights activists, the law provides adequate protective measures and compensation for victims, but the penalties are insufficiently severe and the law does not cover the informal sector, where sexual harassment is most common. According to INSEC, no reports of incidents of sexual harassment were filed under the act during the year. NGOs and government officials stated it was too early to assess implementation of the act, which came into force in February 2015.

Reproductive Rights: Couples and individuals generally could decide the number, spacing, and timing of their children; manage their reproductive health; and have access to the information and means to do so, free from discrimination, coercion, or violence. Due to the prevalence of child marriage, however, many girls faced social pressure to have children before being emotionally ready and before their bodies are able to bear children safely. Contraception was available to both men and women. According to the latest UN Children's Fund (UNICEF)-sponsored Multiple Indicator Cluster Survey conducted in 2014, 47 percent of married women used a modern contraceptive method and 2.5 percent used a traditional method. The 2014 survey indicated that 25 percent of married women had an unmet need for family planning. In addition, awareness of contraception and family planning practices remained limited in remote areas.

According to the World Health Organization, the maternal mortality rate in 2015 was 258 deaths per 100,000 live births, down from 444 deaths in 2005. With more than 75 percent of the national health budget directed towards maternal and childcare, the Ministry of Health endeavored to decrease maternal mortality by providing financial assistance to women seeking skilled delivery care in a health facility and to family planning services. Skilled birth attendants assisted in 56 percent of deliveries according to the 2014 UNICEF-sponsored survey, a 20 percent increase from 2011. Preliminary findings from the Health Facility Survey released in April note that antenatal care services are available to 98 percent of women and services for sexually transmitted infections are available in 74 percent of facilities, on average. Normal childbirth delivery services are available in about half of facilities countrywide, but in only 33 percent of facilities in Terai region.

Discrimination: Although the law provides protections, women faced systemic discrimination, including in employment (see section 7.d.). Discrimination was most common in rural areas where religious and cultural traditions, lack of education, and ignorance of the law remained severe impediments to the exercise of basic rights, such as the right to vote or to hold property in a woman's name. Dalit women in particular faced discrimination by virtue of their gender and caste status. The law grants women equal shares of their parents' inheritance and the right to keep their property after marriage, but many women were not aware of their rights, and others were afraid to challenge existing practice. The law also grants widows complete access and authority to the estate of their deceased husbands; however, traditional attitudes stigmatizing and shunning widows persisted, and communities often ignored the law while the government did not take sufficient measures to enforce it.

The Gender Equality Act adopted in 2006--and more than 60 other laws--contain discriminatory provisions. For example, the law on property rights favors men in land tenancy and the division of family property. The law encourages bigamy by allowing men to remarry without divorcing if the first wife is incapacitated or infertile. The constitution, however, confers rights for women that had not previously received legal protection, including rights equal to those of their spouses in property and family affairs, and special opportunities in education, health, and social security.

The constitution does not allow Nepali women to convey citizenship to their children independent of the citizenship of the child's father (see section 2.d.) and has no specific provision for naturalization of foreign husbands married to Nepali wives.

Children

Birth Registration: According to the constitution, citizenship is derived from one Nepali parent, but a child born to a Nepali woman and a foreign citizen father may obtain citizenship only through naturalization. The constitution also states that children of unknown fathers may obtain citizenship through their mothers. Despite a 2011 Supreme Court decision that permits applicants to seek citizenship through either their father or mother, in practice many have been denied citizenship due to lack of access to local authorities, or lack of awareness of the law by applicants or government officials. This led to difficulty in school admissions. Children whose parents were unknown were considered citizens until their parents were identified. In practice, children without parents, such as street children, faced many bureaucratic hurdles since local authorities often required birth certificates. Those in institutional care could attain citizenship through the guardianship of their respective institutions, but such children sometimes encountered similar obstacles.

Education: The constitution makes primary education compulsory nationwide. In June, the country's Education Act was amended, dividing the education system into Basic Education (grades 1-8), which is free and compulsory, and Secondary Education (grades 9-12), which is neither free nor compulsory. Although government policy had previously provided free primary education for all children between the ages of five and 12, the families of most students bore some costs for examinations and uniforms. The government reported that more than 95 percent of school-age children attended primary schools with gender parity. A gender gap in secondary education, however, persisted with a reported two-thirds of adolescent girls in rural areas not attending school. The literacy rate for women was approximately 57 percent versus 75 percent for men, according to the 2011 census. Some school-age girls did not attend public school due to the absence of separate or proper toilets for girls, reports of violence against girls, early and forced marriage, vulnerabilities posed by geographic distance from home to school, parents' unwillingness to educate girls, cost of schooling, and a lack of trained female teachers. The Department of Education stated that 31 percent of public schools did not have separate toilets for girls. The government continued the process of establishing separate washroom facilities for girls and boys in public schools, according to NGOs.

Government officials stated they were concerned about the impact of the 2015 earthquakes on the education sector. According to the Ministry of Education, about 34,500 classrooms in both public and private schools were destroyed or damaged beyond use. A further 9,986 classrooms sustained minor damage and would need to undergo a thorough structural assessment before they could be used. The earthquake interrupted the education of an estimated two million children. According to the government's Post Disaster Recovery Framework released in May, approximately 6,500 Temporary Learning Centers have been established, and the Ministry of Education stated that the majority of children in earthquake-affected areas were able to access education.

<u>Medical Care</u>: The government provided basic health care free to children and adults although parental discrimination against girls often resulted in impoverished parents giving priority to their sons when seeking medical services.

<u>Child Abuse</u>: Violence against children, including sexual abuse, was reportedly widespread. NGOs stated that in part due to increased awareness, there were more reports of such violence, but there were no reliable estimates on the level of abuse. The government has some mechanisms to respond to child abuse and violence against children, such as special hotlines and the Central Child Welfare Board (CCWB), which has chapters in all 75 districts. In some locations these agencies did not provide adequate support to the NGOs that operated the helplines. According to the NGO Children and Women in Social Service and Human Rights (CWISH), with the exception of allegations of sexual abuse of children, police were insufficiently responsive to reports of child abuse, often mediating the cases instead of pursuing criminal investigations.

The government and NGOs expressed concern about the increased vulnerability of children following the 2015 earthquake. The government took action against abuse of children in areas impacted by the earthquake, but according to NGOs, these measures were insufficient. The police monitored displaced persons camps and the government, in cooperation with NGOs, set up child-friendly spaces in these camps. Child rights activists stated that in informal settlements for displaced persons outside of these camps, large numbers of children not in school were at risk of sexual abuse. More than a year after the earthquake, official estimates were not available of the number of children who remained out of school.

<u>Early and Forced Marriage</u>: The law prohibits marriage for both boys and girls before the age of 20. Families in many areas sometimes forced their young

children to marry. According to a UNICEF survey published in January 2015, the prevalence of early and forced marriage remained high although it had decreased since 2002. Nearly 49 percent of women aged 20 to 49 were married or in a union before age 18 while 15.5 percent of women aged 15 to 49 were married or in a union before age 15. According to the same study, 24.5 percent of women aged 15 to 19 were married or in a union. NGOs expressed concern that the economic impact of the 2015 earthquake could cause the rate of child marriage to increase.

Social, economic, and cultural values promoted the practice of early and forced marriages, especially common in the Dalit and Madhesi communities. The law sets penalties for violations according to the age of the girls involved in child marriage. The penalty includes both a prison sentence and fine with the fees collected going to the girl involved. The Civil Code provides that the government must take action whenever a case of child marriage is filed with authorities.

The government worked with local child rights groups and international donors on the problem of early and forced marriage, although cases often were unreported and law enforcement rarely enforced legislation to prevent early and forced marriage. A number of government child protection and welfare programs, such as scholarship programs targeting girls, attempted to encourage girls to stay in school. In March the government announced a national strategy against child marriage that aims to improve education, economically empower girls, engage men and boys, improve services, and implement existing laws and policies.

Sexual Exploitation of Children: Commercial sexual exploitation of children remained a serious problem, according to NGOs. There were reports of boys and girls surviving on the streets in prostitution and of underage girls employed in dance bars, massage parlors, and cabin restaurants (a type of brothel). The minimum age for consensual sex is 16. The penalties for rape vary according to the age of the victim and the relationship. Conviction for rape can result in 10 to 15 years' imprisonment if the victim is under 10 years of age, eight to 12 years' if the victim is between 10 and 14 years of age, six to 10 years' if the victim is between 14 and 16 years of age, five to eight years' if the victim is between 16 and 20 years of age, and five to seven years if the victim is over 20 years of age. Conviction for attempted rape may be punished by half the penalty provided for rape.

There is no specific law against child pornography, but the Children Act stipulates that no person can involve or use a child for an immoral profession, and photographs cannot be taken or distributed for the purpose of engaging a child in an immoral profession. In addition, photographs that tarnish the character of the child may not be published, exhibited, or distributed. Violators of these sections of the act are subject to fines of up to NRs 10,000 ($100), up to one year in prison, or both. According to the NGO Change Nepal, child pornography cases have also been tried under the Criminal Code as "intent to rape," for which the punishment is also a fine of up to NRs 10,000 ($100) and a sentence of up to one year in prison, or both. Other legal experts stated that if a minor has been sexually assaulted in the production of pornography, the perpetrator can be charged with rape, for which the punishment is up to 15 years in jail depending on the age of the victim.

Displaced Children: A large number of children remained displaced as a result of the 2015 earthquake and its aftershocks (see section 2.d.). The government did not have comprehensive data on children affected by the decade-long Maoist conflict, including the original number of internally displaced and the number who remained displaced. In a 2009 report based on information from 53 districts, the CCWB recorded 9,691 children displaced with both of their parents, 3,930 children who lost one parent, and 1,657 children who lost both parents. Estimates of the number of children who remained displaced varied widely.

Institutionalized Children: Abuse and mistreatment in orphanages and children's homes reportedly was common. An NGO working in this field estimated that approximately 10 percent of registered children's homes met the minimum legal standards of operation. The NGO also reported no significant change in the level or degree of abuse of children compared to previous years. A 2013 study by CWISH showed that few such homes in the Kathmandu Valley met CCWB standards although they provided some basic services. NGOs reported that after the 2015 earthquakes, the CCWB and district child welfare boards showed an increased commitment to conducting inspections and playing an active role in rescuing victims of abuse from children's homes. NGOs stated that the CCWB focused its attention on homes that were in moderate violation of the government's minimum standards rather than homes where more severe physical abuse was reported. They also reported that political factors played a role in determining which homes the CCWB and police targeted for inspections and rescue operations. Additionally, the monitoring did not cover the estimated 50 percent of homes that were unregistered.

An NGO estimated that at least two-thirds of the children in registered homes were not orphans, and the figure for unregistered homes was comparable. The CCWB stated that many children in institutions were inaccurately presented as orphans or destitute to attract the sympathy of fee-paying foreign volunteers and donors.

According to the same NGO, staff sometimes threatened children if they revealed the truth of their parentage, or abused, starved, or otherwise mistreated the children to attract sympathy and financial support. In cases where the CCWB participated in rescue raids, some homes reportedly lost their operating licenses and were prohibited from reopening for five years.

The government took action to prevent and detect institutional abuse of children after the 2015 earthquake, especially following numerous reports of cases in which desperate parents turned over their children to strangers who promised them education and safety in Kathmandu. In response, the government banned the transport of children unaccompanied by a legal guardian to another district without the approval of the District Child Welfare Board (DCWB), increased monitoring of child-welfare homes, and temporarily suspended the registration of new homes. Additionally, the police patrolled displaced persons camps and enhanced monitoring of transportation hubs. Children's rights and anti-trafficking organizations said that the initiatives, which lasted through February, were largely successful but that loopholes existed and the initiatives did not go far enough.

In March the CCWB and Nepal Police raided the children's home Sahara Bal Sudhar Grihar in Kathmandu, rescuing 29 children permanently residing in the facility. According to NGO and government officials, sanitary conditions in the home were extremely poor, there was little adult supervision, the building had unrepaired earthquake damage, children were forced to scavenge for firewood to cook or heat water, and there were no physical security measures in place. Additionally, there was evidence that children were being moved in and out of the home on a regular basis. The families of some children had reportedly paid NRs 40,000 ($400) to enroll them in the home with the expectation they would attend a good school. The DCWB confiscated Sahara Bal Sudhar Grihar's registration certificate, tax certificate, and audit report, and the facility was temporarily shut down.

International Child Abductions: The country is not a party to the 1980 Hague Convention on the Civil Aspects of International Child Abduction. See the Department of State's *Annual Report on International Parental Child Abduction* at travel.state.gov/content/childabduction/en/legal/compliance.html.

Anti-Semitism

There was a small Jewish community in the country, and there were no reports of anti-Semitic acts.

Trafficking in Persons

See the Department of State's *Trafficking in Persons Report* at
www.state.gov/j/tip/rls/tiprpt/.

Persons with Disabilities

The constitution prohibits discrimination based on disability or physical condition
and contains additional rights for persons with disabilities that did not appear in the
2007 interim constitution. These include the right to free higher education for all
physically disabled citizens who are "financially poor" and the provision of special
instructional materials and curricula for persons with vision disabilities.

Although government efforts to enforce laws and regulations to improve rights and
benefits for persons with disabilities have gradually improved, they still were not
effective. In 2012, the Supreme Court ordered the government to do more for
persons with physical and mental disabilities, including providing a monthly
stipend, building shelters, and appointing one social welfare worker in each
district. During the year the government increased social security allowances for
persons with disabilities to NRs 2,000 ($20) per month for those categorized as
"profoundly" disabled, and NRs 600 ($6) for the "severely" disabled. The law
states that other persons with disabilities would receive allowances based on the
availability of funds and the degree of disability. Additionally, the government
provided financial support to sign language interpreters in 20 districts to assist deaf
and hard-of-hearing persons in obtaining government services. The government
allocated NRs 107 million ($1.07 million) for persons with disabilities, including
NRs 69 million ($690,000) for grants to disabled persons' organizations in 15
districts. NGOs reported, however, that although the government attempted to
implement the 2012 Supreme Court order by making budget allocations to
empowerment and development programs, little progress had been made. In
addition to reserving 5 percent of public positions for persons with disabilities and
encouraging the private sector to adopt a similar reservation system, the
government also provided income-generating training to persons with disabilities.
Despite government efforts, persons with disabilities continued to face
discrimination in employment (see section 7.d.).

The Ministry of Women, Children, and Social Welfare was responsible for the
protection of persons with disabilities. Additionally, the Ministry of Education
provided scholarships to help approximately 101,000 children with disabilities

attend public or private schools at the primary and secondary levels. An estimated 60 percent of children with disabilities, particularly those with intellectual or mental, vision, or hearing disabilities, did not attend school. Compared with primary school attendance, relatively few children with disabilities attended higher levels of education, largely due to accessibility problems, school locations, and financial burdens on parents. Although incidents of abuse of children with disabilities reportedly occurred in schools, there were no reports of incidents filed in the courts or with the relevant agencies during the year.

The Ministry of Local Development allocated an estimated 1 to 2 percent of the budget of local development agencies for disability programs. Some NGOs working with persons with disabilities received funding from the government, but most persons with disabilities relied almost exclusively on family members for assistance.

There are no restrictions in law on the rights of persons with disabilities to vote and participate in civic affairs or to access the judicial system. According to the Ministry of Women, Children, and Social Welfare, however, there were obstacles to exercising these rights, especially the lack of accessibility to public facilities. The government also reserved 5 percent of public positions for persons with disabilities.

Access to mental health services was available in larger cities, but the Ministry of Women, Children, and Social Welfare decreased its allocation for mental health organizations during the year from NRs 1.5 million to 1 million ($15,000 to $10,000).

National/Racial/Ethnic Minorities

The law provides that each community shall have the right "to preserve and promote its language, script, and culture" and to operate schools at the primary level in its native language. The government generally upheld these provisions. There are more than 125 caste and ethnic groups, some of which are considered indigenous nationalities, speaking more than 120 different languages.

Discrimination against lower castes and some ethnic groups, including in employment (see section 7.d.), was widespread and especially common in the Terai region and in rural areas.

Caste-based discrimination is illegal, and the government outlawed the public shunning of Dalits and made an effort to protect the rights of other disadvantaged castes. The constitution expands the prohibition of the practice of untouchability contained in the 2007 interim constitution to cover private spaces and stipulates special legal protections for Dalits in education, health care, and housing. It also established the National Dalit Commission as a constitutional body to strengthen protection and promote the rights of Dalits.

According to the Nepal National Dalit Social Welfare Organization, government progress in reducing discrimination remained limited in rural areas, and police were reluctant to investigate incidents of alleged discrimination, often preferring to mediate such cases. Media reported several incidents of Dalits living in areas affected by the 2015 earthquakes facing a disadvantage in receiving aid and reconstruction supplies compared with upper-caste communities nearby. NGOs stated that the practice was not widespread, however, and that local and international NGOs engaged in relief and reconstruction made efforts to ensure there was no caste discrimination in the distribution of aid or reconstruction materials.

Resistance to intercaste marriage sometimes resulted in ostracism or forced expulsion from the community, according to media reports and NGOs advocating for Dalit rights. Media reports also covered incidents in which Dalits were barred from entering temples and teashops and sharing water sources, and they occasionally suffered violence in such situations. NGOs said that the frequency of such incidents continued to decline slightly, possibly due to improved awareness of the antidiscrimination law, but such instances persisted. In one case of intercaste marriage, Ajit Mijar, a member of the Dalit community, married Kalpana Parjuli on July 9. On July 14, Mijar's body was found hanged in Dhading district. Although the case was initially reported as a suicide, Mijar's family suspected he had been killed deliberately and filed a case with the police. Dalit NGOs stated that the police were unresponsive and did not conduct a thorough investigation of the case. The NHRC, jointly with the National Dalit Commission and the Nepal Police, was monitoring the investigation.

In urban areas, particularly in the Kathmandu Valley, better education and higher levels of prosperity slowly reduced caste distinctions and increased opportunities for lower socioeconomic groups. Members of better-educated, urban-oriented castes continued to dominate politics and senior administrative and military ranks and control a disproportionate share of natural resources, and Dalits continued to report exclusion from local and national politics.

Indigenous People

The government recognized 59 ethnic/caste groups as indigenous nationalities, comprising approximately 36 percent of the population. Although some communities were comparatively privileged, many faced unequal access to government resources and political institutions and linguistic, religious, and cultural discrimination. Some NGOs stated that indigenous people, whose settlements were disproportionately damaged by the 2015 earthquakes, were discriminated against in the quality and quantity of aid and reconstruction materials they received.

Conflicts between indigenous groups and government authorities over control of local resources and the distribution of benefits from development projects sometimes occurred. Some disputes arose over interpretation of the country's obligations under International Labor Organization Convention 169, which indigenous groups maintained granted them exclusive rights over natural resources.

According to AF's 2015 report on torture, a slightly higher rate of torture occurred among detainees identified as indigenous than among the overall population sampled. An Amnesty International report published in July accused police of subjecting members of the Tharu community in Kailali district to arbitrary arrests, torture, other ill-treatment, and coercion of some community members into signing forced confessions following the killings by protesters of eight security personnel and a child in Tikapur in August 2015.

Acts of Violence, Discrimination, and Other Abuses Based on Sexual Orientation and Gender Identity

No laws criminalize same-sex sexual activity, and lesbian, gay, bisexual, transgender, and intersex (LGBTI) persons actively advocated for their rights. The constitution contains provisions outlining protections for LGBTI persons, but LGBTI activists continued to press for further legislation to increase protections for gender and sexual minorities.

In 2007, the Supreme Court directed the government to enact laws to protect LGBTI persons' fundamental rights, enable third-gender citizenship, and amend laws that were sexually discriminatory. Implementation of the 2007 decision was initially slow, but in 2013 the Home Ministry started issuing citizenship certificates with an "other" gender category for those applying for citizenship. In 2015 the Home Ministry started issuing passports with an "other" gender designation. The constitution enshrines the right of citizens to choose their gender identity on citizenship documents, according to human rights lawyers. The Ministry of Women, Children, and Social Welfare increased its budget for LGBTI-focused programs from NRs 600,000 ($6,000) to NRs 1.5 million ($15,000) for awareness programs, income generation training, and other LGBTI community needs as determined by two major LGBTI advocacy NGOs, Blue Diamond Society (BDS) and Inclusive Forum Nepal. According to local LGBTI advocacy groups, the government did not provide equal opportunity to LGBTI persons in education, health care, or employment (see section 7.d.). Additionally, LGBTI advocacy groups stated that some LGBTI persons faced difficulties in registering for citizenship, particularly in rural areas.

According to local LGBTI rights NGOs, harassment and abuse of LGBTI persons by private citizens and government officials declined during the year, especially in urban areas, although incidents still occurred. Several NGOs praised the government, specifically the Ministry of Women, Children, and Social Welfare, for taking greater initiative in organizing LGBTI-related trainings and sensitivity programs.

LGBTI rights groups reported that gender and sexual minorities faced harassment from police during the year. According to BDS, police continued to target transgender sex workers, subjecting them to as much as 25 days' detention without charge under the Public Offense Act. Although the Nepal Police HRC did not document any allegations of harassment of LGBTI persons, the NGO Inclusive Forum Nepal reported that in February, two gay men were attacked in Makwanpur district. When they reported the incident to the police, the police refused to register the case and scolded the couple for inappropriate behavior. The HRC confirmed that some low-level harassment occurred because many citizens held negative views of LGBTI persons. The HRC added that the Nepal Police were not immune to such social prejudices. The HRC continued to conduct LGBTI rights training and worked with LGBTI NGOs to minimize and prevent harassment.

HIV and AIDS Social Stigma

There was no official discrimination against persons who provided HIV-prevention services or against high-risk groups that could spread HIV/AIDS.

Societal discrimination and stigma against persons with HIV decreased but remained common, according to NGOs. In the most recent Demographic and Health Survey for the country, 30.7 percent of women and 24.9 percent of men reported discriminatory attitudes towards those with HIV.

According to NGOs, social acceptance of people with HIV increased, largely due to government-sponsored awareness programs for health-care workers and volunteers, media, police, teachers and students, local leaders, and community members.

Most health-care facilities that provided HIV-related services did so without significant stigma or discrimination, but there were reported incidents of hampered access for persons with HIV to education and health care, especially surgical and dental care, and treatment for pregnant women. The government approved a National HIV/AIDS Strategy that focuses on increasing medical services to HIV-infected persons and reducing social discrimination.

According to the National Association of People Living with HIV and AIDS in Nepal, a national network, a women's group forced an individual employed at the local health post in Kailali district to leave his job and the village when they discovered he was HIV-positive. The coordinated response by NGOs and district health officials, including training on reducing stigma and discrimination, ultimately led the community to welcome the individual back to the village and his position.

Other Societal Violence or Discrimination

During the widespread civil unrest, protests, and general strikes in the mid-western hills and Terai region from August 2015 to February 2016, there were reports of demonstrators attacking those who opposed ethnic Madhesi and Tharu political movements. Specifically, THRDA reported that on January 21, around 200 young people of hill origin traveled on buses to Morang district in the Terai and verbally and physically attacked local residents of Dainya Village Development Committee with rods, batons, and beer bottles. When thousands of local Madhesis chased the young people toward a group of police officers, the police took the young people away in a police van. The local residents accused the police of protecting the instigators of the violence, and torched two of the buses on which the hill-based youths had arrived. There were allegations that some of the violent "demonstrators" were criminals paid by persons with a political agenda.

Section 7. Worker Rights

a. Freedom of Association and the Right to Collective Bargaining

The law provides for the right of workers to form and join unions of their choice, except those deemed by the government to be subversive or seditious organizations. Freedom of association extends to workers in both the formal and informal sectors. Noncitizens cannot be elected as trade union officials. In the formal sector, noncitizens are allowed to work exclusively in managerial positions. Due to laws that prevent managers from forming unions, noncitizens in effect do not have the right to form unions. In the informal sector, unions are uncommon, and noncitizens cannot gain membership. Local workers have the right to strike and bargain collectively, except for employees in 16 essential services, including public transportation, banking, security, and health care. Members of the armed forces, police, and government officials at the undersecretary level or higher are also prohibited from taking part in union activities. In the private sector, employees in managerial positions are not permitted to join unions.

The law stipulates that unions must represent at least 25 percent of workers in a given workplace to be considered representative. The minimum requirement does not prohibit the formation of unofficial union groups, which may call strikes and enter into direct negotiation with the government. Workers in the informal sector may also form unions, but many workers were not aware of these rights.

The law also protects union representatives from adverse legal action arising from their official union duties, including collective bargaining, and prohibits antiunion discrimination. Workers dismissed for engaging in union activities can seek reinstatement by filing a complaint in labor court or with the Department of Labor, which has semijudicial and mediation authority. Most cases are settled through mediation. By law, employers can fire workers only under limited conditions and only after three instances of misconduct. The law stipulates that participation in a strike that does not meet legal requirements constitutes misconduct, for which the consequences are suspension or termination of employment.

To conduct a legal strike, 51 percent of a union's membership must vote in favor in a secret ballot, and unions are required to give 30 days' notice before striking. If the union is unregistered, does not have majority support, or calls a strike prior to issuing 30 days' notice, the strike is considered illegal.

The government was unable to enforce applicable laws fully, since resources, inspections, and remediations were inadequate and penalties for violations were insufficient to deter violations. Administrative and judicial procedures were subject to lengthy delays and appeals.

Freedom of association and the right to collective bargaining were generally respected. Although the government restricted strikes in essential services, workers in hospitals, education services, and the transportation sector called numerous strikes during the year and did not face any legal penalties. Many unions had links to political parties and did not operate independently from them.

The government did not interfere in the functioning of workers' organizations or threaten union leaders. Strikes in essential service sectors such as hospitals, despite being prohibited, continued to take place. Many doctors and medical professionals at Tribhuvan University Teaching Hospital (TUTH), the country's premier medical education institution, supported the eighth hunger strike in recent years by Dr. Govinda KC, who demanded action against officials allegedly involved in improperly granting affiliation to private medical colleges and compromising the quality of medical education. KC also demanded the impeachment of Commission for the Investigation of Abuses of Authority Chief Karki. Some TUTH staff joined KC's strike in July, accusing the government of not implementing regulatory measures agreed upon during a previous strike. The 16-day hunger strike ended with a deal between KC and government officials. When the government failed to implement the deal, KC carried out another 12-day hunger strike in September and October.

b. Prohibition of Forced or Compulsory Labor

The law prohibits all forms of forced or compulsory labor and provides penalties ranging from one to 20 years in prison and fines of up to NRs 200,000 ($2,000). The law does not criminalize the recruitment, transportation, harboring, or receipt of persons by force, fraud, or coercion for the purpose of forced labor. The government made significant efforts to comply with minimum standards for the elimination of trafficking despite limited resources, but the country continued to be a source, transit, and destination for men, women, and children who were subjected to forced labor.

Government enforcement of the laws against bonded labor was uneven, and social reintegration of victims remained difficult. Resources, inspections, and remediation were inadequate, and penalties for violations were insufficient to deter violations. The government provided financial, material, and other social welfare benefits to more than 26,000 "Kamaiyas" (bonded agricultural laborers of Tharu ethnicity who were freed in 2000). This included NRs 10,000 ($100) per family to purchase materials for the construction of homes. Many former Kamaiya families nevertheless continued to reside on riverbanks and barren plots of land under poor living conditions, with limited employment opportunities and little access to education.

In 2013, the government recommitted to abolishing the already illegal practice of Kamlaris, girls of Tharu ethnicity in bonded domestic labor. The government allocated NRs 120 million ($1.2 million) for the education of former Kamlaris, but authorities did not spend the full amount.

Also see the Department of State's *Trafficking in Persons Report* at www.state.gov/j/tip/rls/tiprpt/.

c. Prohibition of Child Labor and Minimum Age for Employment

The law establishes 14 as the minimum age for work and 16 as the minimum age for hazardous work, and it mandates acceptable working conditions for children. Employers must maintain separate records of laborers between the ages of 14 and 16. The law prohibits employment of children in factories, mines, and 60 other categories of hazardous work and limits children between the ages of 16 and 18 to a 36-hour workweek (six hours a day between 6 a.m. and 6 p.m., six days a week). The law, which was not fully implemented, also establishes penalties of up to two years in prison and a fine up to NRs 100,000 ($1,000) for those who unlawfully employ children.

The Department of Labor, which is responsible for enforcing child labor laws and practices, had a weak enforcement record. The Department of Labor conducted most of its labor inspections in the formal sector while nearly all child labor occurred in the informal sector. As of August, the department reported that only five of its 12 factory inspector positions responsible for regular monitoring were filled. Some of these positions were vacant due to regular rotation of civil servants, and resources devoted to enforcement were limited. In 2015, the Department of Labor created five Senior Labor Officer positions in industry-heavy districts, but as of August, the positions were all vacant. There is a broad range of laws and policies designed to combat and eventually eliminate child labor. Penalties range from a NRs 10,000 ($100) fine and one year in prison to a NRs 200,000 ($2,000) fine and 20 years' imprisonment.

Child labor occurred in agriculture, domestic service, portering, recycling, and transportation; the worst abuses were reported in brick kilns, the stone-breaking industry, the carpet sector, embroidery factories, and the entertainment sector. In the informal sector children worked long hours in unhealthy environments, carried heavy loads, were at risk of sexual exploitation, and at times suffered from numerous health problems (see section 6, Children). Government officials stated they were concerned that the economic impact of the 2015 earthquakes would spark an increased risk of child labor, but no official data was available as of August.

In 2016 Lalitpur submetropolitan city in the Kathmandu Valley expanded its "green flag campaign" to eliminate child labor. Under the campaign, local NGOs working in the field of child rights placed a green flag at every house that did not employ child labor. NGOs also coordinated with local government and police to rescue children working as household servants.

According to the 2008 Nepal Labor Force Survey, the most recent data available, the labor-force participation rate was 13.4 percent for children between the ages of five and nine and 52.7 percent for children between 10 and 14.

Also see the Department of Labor's *Findings on the Worst Forms of Child Labor* at www.dol.gov/ilab/reports/child-labor/findings/.

d. Discrimination with Respect to Employment and Occupation

The 2007 Interim Constitution prohibited discrimination on the basis of religion, race, sex, caste, tribe, social origin, language, or ideological conviction. It also stipulated that the government could make special provisions for the protection, empowerment or advancement of women, Dalits, indigenous peoples, persons with disabilities, and those "who belong to a class which is economically, socially or culturally backward." The 2015 constitution added a general prohibition on discrimination on the basis of disability and physical and health conditions. It also added gender and sexual minorities to the categories eligible for special measures on protection, empowerment, and advancement. On employment specifically, the 2015 constitution gives women the right to special opportunities and gives ethnic minorities, persons with disabilities, Muslims, and gender and sexual minorities the right to serve in state bodies though a principle of inclusion. It also states that there will be special legal provisions for Dalits in employment, including in public service. Labor regulations prohibit discrimination in payment or remuneration based on gender.

There are no provisions in the constitution, law, or regulations prohibiting discrimination, including labor discrimination, or discrimination based on color, age, national origin or citizenship, HIV-positive status, or other communicable disease.

Despite constitutional and legal protections, discrimination in employment and occupation occurred with respect to gender, caste, ethnicity, national origin, citizenship, disability, religion, sexual orientation and gender identity, and HIV-positive status. Such discrimination was most common in the informal sector, where monitoring by the government and human rights organizations was weak or absent and those in disadvantaged categories had little leverage or recourse. In the formal sector, labor discrimination generally took the form of upper-caste men without disabilities being favored in hiring, promotions, and transfers. In the public sector, such discrimination was also based on personal affiliation and reportedly occurred in many instances with the tacit understanding of political leaders.

Although the law requires equal pay for equal work for men and women, the government did not implement those provisions, in particular in many state industries. To be eligible for government jobs, Nepali national origin or citizenship is mandatory, and dual nationals are excluded. A fixed-term employment of a foreign national under contractual arrangements or as a consultant, however, is permitted. Labor laws limit hiring foreign nationals in fully owned or joint-venture foreign enterprises.

The government used a mandatory 5 percent public employment quota to hire persons with disabilities during the year, primarily as teachers. The government also attempted to implement this quota system on a voluntary basis in the private sector and during the year began conducting free classes to help persons with disabilities prepare for public-service exams. Nevertheless, according to government officials and disability rights advocates, the overall rate of employment of persons with disabilities did not increase significantly. In the private sector, large numbers of persons with disabilities claimed they were denied work opportunities or dismissed due to their conditions. In all sectors employees with disabilities reported other forms of discriminatory treatment.

According to the Nepal National Dalit Social Welfare Organization, the government made little progress in implementing antidiscrimination legal provisions to ensure employment opportunities for lower-caste individuals in both the public and private sectors. There was no comprehensive data on this.

The government committed to take action for the economic empowerment of gender and sexual minorities and other marginalized groups in its fourth five-year National Plan of Action on Human Rights (2014-19). Local LGBTI advocacy organizations, however, stated there was a lack of implementation. There were no reliable data on discrimination against LGBTI persons in various sectors, but activists reported it was common for gender and sexual minorities to be denied promotions and competitive opportunities within the security services and athletics. There were some reports of individuals losing their jobs when their employers or coworkers discovered their HIV-positive status. According to a development NGO working in the area of HIV/AIDS, there was evidence that a longstanding government policy to foster acceptance of persons with HIV and respect for their rights in the workplace had not been implemented effectively.

e. Acceptable Conditions of Work

The government increased the minimum wage for unskilled laborers in February from NRs 8,000 to 9,700 ($80 to $97) per month. For workers in the tea industry, the minimum wage was increased in July from NRs 6375 ($64) to 7075 ($71) per month, with an additional allowance of NRs 30 ($.30) per day. The minimum wage exceeded the official poverty line of NRs 52 ($.53) per day, but it was barely sufficient to meet subsistence needs. This was particularly the case in the aftermath of the 2015 earthquakes and constitution-related political unrest when inflation of consumer goods was high.

Minimum-wage laws apply to both the formal sector (which accounted for approximately 10 percent of the workforce) and the informal sector, but implementation was stronger in the formal sector. As per an understanding reached between the Joint Trade Union Coordination Center (a common forum of 11 trade unions), the Federation of Nepalese Chambers of Commerce and Industry, and the Ministry of Labor and Employment, the minimum wage should be revised every two years. Under the understanding, the wage increase was due in May 2015, but due to the earthquakes and subsequent political unrest, the revision was delayed eight months.

The law stipulates a 48-hour workweek, with one day off per week and one-half hour of rest per five hours worked. The law limits overtime to no more than four hours in a day and 20 hours per week, with a 50 percent overtime premium per hour. Excessive compulsory overtime is prohibited. Employees are also entitled to paid public holiday leave, sick leave, annual leave, maternity leave, bereavement leave, and other special leave. The law provides adequate occupational health and safety standards and establishes other benefits, such as a provident fund, housing facilities, day-care arrangements for establishments with more than 50 female workers, and maternity benefits.

The Ministry of Labor and Employment reported that most factories in the formal sector complied with laws on minimum wage and hours of work, but implementation varied in the informal sector, including in agriculture and domestic servitude. The ministry employed up to 12 factory inspectors for the entire country, who also acted as labor and occupational health and safety inspectors.

Implementation and enforcement of occupational health and safety standards were minimal, and the Ministry of Labor and Employment considered it the most neglected area of labor law enforcement. The ministry found violations across sectors, including in construction, mining, transportation, agriculture, and factory work.

The government has not created the necessary regulatory or administrative structures to enforce occupational safety and health provisions. The Ministry of Labor and Employment did not have a specific office dedicated to occupational safety and health, nor did it have inspectors specifically trained in this area. Penalties were insufficient to deter violations. Although the law authorizes factory inspectors to order employers to rectify unsafe conditions, enforcement of safety standards remained minimal, and monitoring was weak. Accurate data on workplace fatalities and accidents were not available. Labor law and regulations do not specify that workers can remove themselves from situations that endanger health or safety without jeopardizing their employment.

The government regulated labor contracting, or "manpower," agencies recruiting workers for overseas jobs, and penalized fraudulent recruitment practices. The government remained committed to the free-visa, free-ticket scheme introduced in 2015. Some government officials were complicit in falsifying travel documents and overlooking recruiting violations by labor contractors. The myriad unregistered and unregulated labor "brokers" and intermediaries, who were often trusted members of the community, complicated effective monitoring of recruitment practices. Workers were also encouraged to register and pay a fee to the Foreign Employment Promotion Board, which tracked migrant workers and provided some compensation for workers whose rights were violated.

The government required contracts for workers going abroad to be translated into Nepali and instituted provisions whereby workers must attend a pre-departure orientation program. During the orientation workers are made aware of their rights and legal recourse, should their rights be violated. The effectiveness of the initiatives remained questionable since workers who went overseas often skipped the mandatory training, and many companies issued pre-departure orientation certificates for a small fee and failed to deliver the training. Nepali migrant workers abroad often continued to face exploitive conditions.

There were large numbers of workers in the informal sector although no data were available to confirm the size of the informal economy with precision. According to the Nepal Labor Force Survey, in 2008 an estimated 2.15 million persons ages 15 and over were employed in the nonagricultural informal sector (70 percent of total nonagricultural employment at that time).

The law provides for protection of workers from work situations that endanger their health and safety, but in small and cottage industries located in small towns and villages, employers sometimes forced workers to work in such situations or risk losing their jobs.